Disney MOANA
The Pacific Islands
A *Moana* Discovery Book

By Paul Dichter

Special thanks to Niuafolau Dionne Fonoti of the
National University of Samoa

Lerner Publications • Minneapolis

Lerner Publications Company
A division of Lerner Publishing Group, Inc.
241 First Avenue North
Minneapolis, MN 55401 USA

For reading levels and more information, look up this
title at www.lernerbooks.com.

Main body text set in Mikado 12/20.
Typeface provided by HVD Fonts.

Library of Congress Cataloging-in-Publication Data

The Cataloging-in-Publication Data for *The Pacific
    Islands: A* Moana *Discovery Book* is on file at the
    Library of Congress.
ISBN 978-1-5415-3258-8 (lib. bdg.)
ISBN 978-1-5415-3276-2 (pbk.)
ISBN 978-1-5415-3264-9 (eb pdf)

Manufactured in the United States of America
1-44848-35718-1/23/2018

CONTENTS

WELCOME TO THE PACIFIC ISLANDS!

Welcome! Let's explore the amazing place Moana and her friends call home: the **Pacific Islands!**

Pacific Ocean

Where in the World?

The **Pacific Ocean** is the largest and deepest ocean in the world. It covers more than one-third of the globe! The Pacific Islands are in the Pacific Ocean. The Pacific Islands are also known as **Oceania**. All kinds of plants, animals, and people call Oceania home.

Meet the Islanders

Meet Moana, her family, and her friends. Gramma Tala may have a tale or two to tell. Maui, the shape-shifter and demigod of the wind and sea, is here too. He may be a bit boastful, but he is—after all—a hero. And let's not forget Heihei, Moana's silly rooster, or her pet pig Pua. They will be your guides as you venture on your quest to learn more about the Pacific Islands.

What You'll Learn

In this book you'll discover some of the plants and animals of the Pacific Islands. You'll find out what many Pacific Islanders eat and drink. You'll learn about the clothes many Pacifc Islanders wear and the music they might play. We'll talk about **wayfinding**, the special way Pacific Islanders found their way from island to island. And you'll learn some of the stories they passed down from generation to generation.

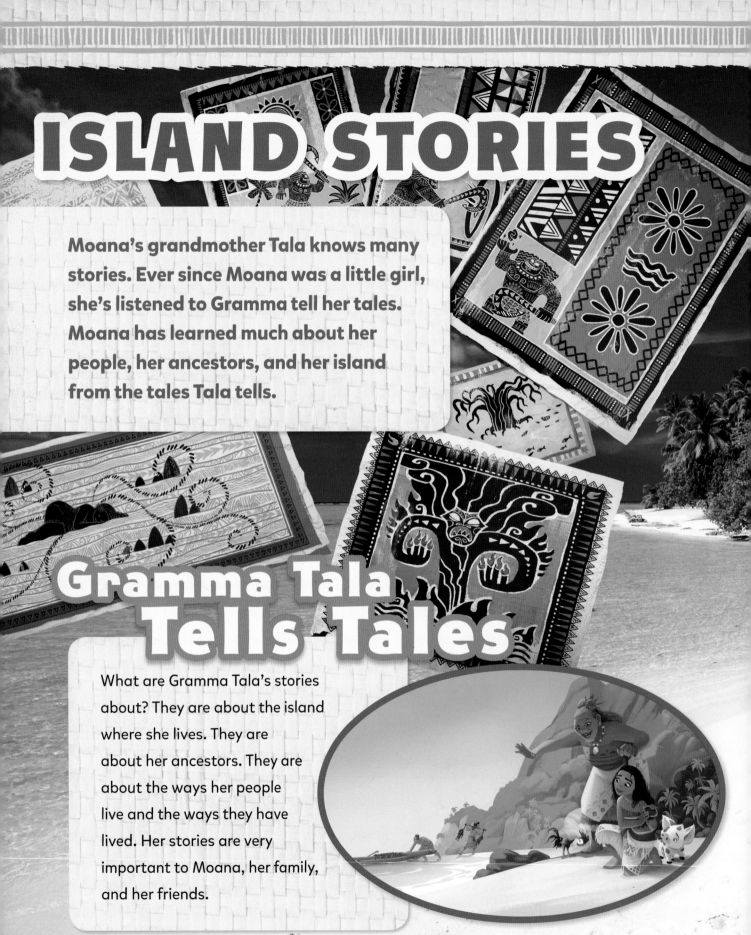

ISLAND STORIES

Moana's grandmother Tala knows many stories. Ever since Moana was a little girl, she's listened to Gramma tell her tales. Moana has learned much about her people, her ancestors, and her island from the tales Tala tells.

Gramma Tala Tells Tales

What are Gramma Tala's stories about? They are about the island where she lives. They are about her ancestors. They are about the ways her people live and the ways they have lived. Her stories are very important to Moana, her family, and her friends.

Oral History

We don't always know the exact dates and times for events from the past in the Pacific Islands. This is because stories in the past weren't written down as they are now. Instead, they were spoken out loud. Stories were told by storytellers like Gramma Tala. These storytellers passed the stories down to their children and their children's children. This is called **oral history**. This kind of storytelling connects people to one another and to their past.

Many Islands, Many Stories

The Pacific Islands are rich with stories. There are many countries in the Pacific Islands. Each has its own language. While many of these languages and stories are connected, they are also different. Each island has its own culture and its own tales to tell.

THE PACIFIC ISLANDS

Moana lives on an island. There are more than twenty thousand islands in the Pacific Ocean. Only some of these islands have people on them.

The Three -nesias!

The Pacific Islands are divided into three groups: **Melanesia**, which means "black islands"; **Micronesia**, which means "small islands"; and **Polynesia**, which means "many islands." The "nesia" part of the names come from a Greek word that means "island."

- Micronesia
- Melanesia
- Polynesia

Samoa and Tonga

Two of the countries in Polynesia are **Samoa** and **Tonga**. People have lived on those islands for more than two thousand years. Samoa means "sacred center." Tonga is made up of 171 islands! Fewer than half of the islands in Tonga have people on them.

Samoa

Tonga

Hawai'i and New Zealand

Hawai'i

New Zealand

Two of the last islands that were settled in Polynesia are **Hawai'i** and **New Zealand**. Hawai'i is in the northern part of Polynesia. New Zealand is very far south. Hawai'i is part of the United States. The first settlers traveled over 2,000 miles (3,200 km) by **canoe** to reach Hawai'i. Early Pacific settlers made an even longer trip to New Zealand about twelve hundred years ago. They named their home **Aotearoa**. This name is still used today.

FLORA OF THE ISLANDS

Moana's fictional island, Motunui, is full of plants, trees, and flowers. All the plants in a place are called the **flora**. There's a huge variety of flora in the Pacific Islands. Because there are so many islands, there are many different **climates** and types of flora.

Rain Forests

Some islands have a dry side and a wet side. On the wet side of many islands, there are mountains. And on many of these islands with mountains, there are also **rain forests**. **Fiji**, Samoa, and **Tahiti** all have rain forests. Because it rains so much, rain forests are home to many different plants and trees.

Grasslands

On the dry side of some islands, there are **grasslands**. Grasslands can often be found where there is less wind. Hawai'i and Fiji have grasslands. Grasslands are home to many kinds of grasses, but they have few trees.

So Many Plants!

Three of the most common plants in the Pacific Islands are **ferns**, **mangroves**, and **coconut palms**. Ferns are some of the oldest plants on Earth! They grow in forests and near the shore too. Mangroves are trees that live right next to the ocean. Unlike most trees, they can survive in salt water. Coconut palm trees have coconuts on them . . . of course! They can grow to be almost 100 feet (30 m) tall.

Ferns

Mangroves

Coconut palms

FAUNA OF THE ISLANDS

Moana's animal friends, Pua and Heihei, are part of the **fauna** on Moana's island home. All the animals in a place are called the fauna. Many kinds of animals live on different islands of the Pacific.

Native and Non-Native Animals

The first Pacific Islanders brought many animals with them when they explored. These are called **non-native** animals. Animals that are originally from a place are called **native** animals. Bats called flying foxes are one kind of animal native to Fiji. What about Pua and Heihei? Pigs and chickens were brought to the islands thousands of years ago.

Fijian flying foxes

Collared kingfisher

Birds

Many kinds of birds are native to the Pacific Islands. They include parrots, doves, kingfishers, herons, swallows, and warblers. Many of these birds are **seabirds**.

Sea Creatures

Many sea creatures live in the waters around the Pacific Islands. Sea turtles, dolphins, and whales live off the coast of Fiji. Clown fish, crabs, and tuna swim in the waters of the **Marshall Islands**. Manta rays, squid, and sea lions can be found by Hawai'i. The ocean is full of life.

Butterfly fish

FOOD AND DRINK

What do Pacific Islanders eat? What do they drink? Is it similar to what you eat and drink?

Fishing and Farming

Many islanders fish for food. The first Pacific Islanders got much of their food from the ocean. Even today Pacific Islanders still use canoes to fish off the coast. Islanders also grow their food. Villages farm yams, breadfruit, and taro. They also grow many kinds of fruit, including bananas, mangoes, and pineapples.

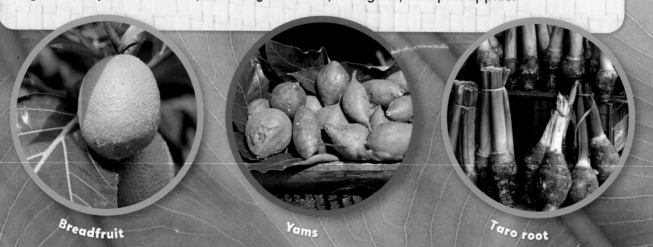

Breadfruit

Yams

Taro root

The Amazing Coconut

The coconut is one of the most important fruits in all the Pacific Islands. Islanders use every single part of the coconut. They drink the water inside the coconut. They eat the coconut's meat. They turn the meat into coconut milk and cook with it. They use the husks to make rope and string. They use the shells to make bowls.

Drinking Water

Where do Pacific Islanders get their drinking water? Not from the ocean. The water from the ocean is too salty. Many islands have freshwater lakes, waterfalls, and pools. Many islanders collect rainwater and save it. Sometimes the only freshwater on an island is found underground.

ISLAND HOUSES

What kind of houses did Pacific Islanders in Moana's time live in? Do their homes look like yours?

The *Fale*

In Tonga and Samoa, a house is called a *fale*. Early Samoans and Tongans built *fale* using only what they had on the island. Samoans used wood from *poumuli* trees to hold up a roof made of coconut leaves sewn together with rope. The rope was made of—you guessed it—coconut! They didn't use nails or glue. Everything they used to build the *fale* was local and natural. Some Samoans still build houses this way.

Fale in the Village

There are different kinds of *fale* in a traditional Samoan village. Many villages had a big meeting house. This big *fale* is for ceremonies and meetings. There's also a separate *fale* for cooking food. Most villages even have a *fale* for guests.

The Perfect Shelter

Did you notice that the *fale* has no walls? Can you guess why? It has to do with the weather. It can be very hot in the islands. The open shape of the *fale* keeps it cool inside. The breeze passes through the house. The roof provides shade and shelter from the rain.

The Roof

Here's one more fun fact about *fale*. Look at the design of the roof. It looks like an upside-down boat. Island boats were often built the same way as the roofs, using the same materials!

ISLAND CLOTHES

What kind of clothes did early Pacific Islanders like Moana wear? What about leaders like Chief Tui? What about on special occasions? It depends on the island.

Tapa Cloth

Many early Pacific Islanders wore clothes made of **tapa** cloth. Fiji, Samoa, and Tonga were some of the places that made tapa. Tapa is made out of tree bark. Villagers softened the bark by soaking it in water and beating it. Often they would decorate the tapa with beautiful designs.

Special Occasions

During certain ceremonies, many Pacific Islanders wore **headdresses**. The headdresses were mostly made from plants, feathers, and shells from the island.

Weaving with coconut leaves

Use What You Have!

Pacific Islanders made everything they needed with what they had on the island. In Samoa, islanders created clothes from softened tree bark and wove clothes out of leaves. They decorated the clothing using dyes made from the nuts, seeds, juices, and sap of plants on the island.

EXPRESS YOURSELF!

Gramma Tala, Tui, and Moana don't just wear tapa. They wear necklaces too! What about Moana's friend Maui? He has **tattoos**. Let's look at some of the ways Pacific Islanders express themselves.

Jewelry

Some Pacific Islanders wear jewelry. Their ancestors made it out of local island material. Shells, bone, seeds, wood, and coconut were commonly used. Sometimes they would wear jewelry just for special ceremonies. Sometimes it was worn to show wealth or power. Some kinds of necklaces were worn only by **chiefs**.

Masks

On many Melanesian islands, people made masks. These would be worn during special ceremonies. In **Papua New Guinea**, only men wore masks. Some masks were made to be worn. Some were hung in houses or on the front of canoes.

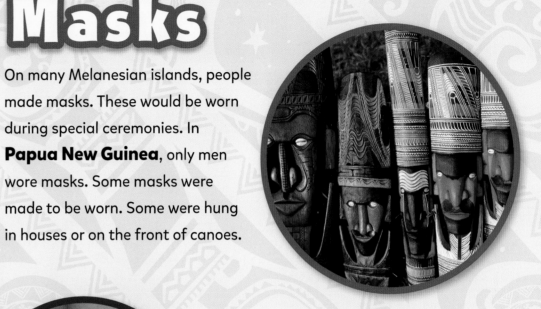

Tattoos

On many Pacific Islands, tattoos were and still are a very important part of the culture. Samoans have been tattooing for more than two thousand years. Tattoos are done by hand using a tool made from a sharp tooth or a row of metal teeth. Tattooing a young man or woman is a special event. The tattoos are very painful. It is thought that getting tattooed shows you are brave.

ANCIENT WISDOM OF THE ISLANDS

The first Pacific Islanders made drawings, carvings, and statues. But they didn't think of them as just art. These objects were more than decoration. They often had ceremonial or religious meaning. They were created to help tell stories and remember special events.

The *Moai*

These are the ***moai***. They are statues found on **Rapa Nui**. Rapa Nui is also called **Easter Island**. The moai were carved hundreds of years ago. The tallest statue is almost 33 feet (10 m) high! The moai may represent the ancestors of the sculptors.

Ha'amonga 'a Maui

This is a monument in Tonga called **Ha'amonga 'a Maui**. That means "Burden of Maui." The monument is made of three huge stone slabs. Each one weighs more than 40,000 pounds (18,000 kg)! It is almost a thousand years old. It may have been built to measure time using the sun.

Petroglyphs

Petroglyphs are rock drawings. The **Marquesas Islands** have many petroglyphs. There are drawings of turtles, canoes, and people. We have no idea how old they are.

MUSIC

Music is a big part of Moana's life. She first beat a drum when she was a little girl. Pacific Islanders have deep musical cultures.

Pahu

Lali

Rattles

Drums!

In Polynesia, a drum called the **pahu** is made from coconut trees and sharkskin. In Fiji, **lalis**—long drums made from logs—are common. In Papua New Guinea, many musicians played **rattles**. These are made from seeds, leaves, and shells. Music was and still is a big part of many ceremonies and dances.

Singing!

Pacific Islanders have been singing for thousands of years. They sang as part of many religious ceremonies. Sometimes they used song to pass stories down from one generation to the next.

In the Pacific, songs have always been a way to document important events.

Instruments!

What other instruments are played in the Pacific Islands? Some Polynesians play the **nose flute**. Other islanders play **conch shells** or **panpipes**. In recent times, the guitar and ukulele have become popular instruments to use in Pacific Island music.

Nose flute

Conch shell

Panpipes

VILLAGE LIFE

Moana's father, Tui, is the chief of her village. What does it mean to be chief? What was it like living in a village like Moana's?

Village Chiefs

On many of the Pacific Islands, villages were made up of groups of families. The families are very close. In Samoa, each village is led by chiefs. Chiefs are in charge of their own families and all the other families in the village. The chiefs don't act alone. Everyone in the village helps make important decisions.

Ceremonies

A chief has a lot of responsibilities. One of them is leading village ceremonies. Each village is like its own country. Villages have lots of events on the **malae**, or village square. They can be religious ceremonies. Some events can be about problems villagers are having. They can also be weddings and celebrations.

Celebration in Vanuatu

Honored Guests

In Samoa, guests from other villages are welcomed with open arms. When guests arrive, the ceremonies begin. The chief or his children may put on a headdress or **tuiga** as part of a welcome ceremony. The women of the village march toward the guesthouse. They sing and dance while they do this. They bring the guests the best food they have. They give speeches, sing songs, and exchange gifts.

THE IMPORTANCE OF THE OCEAN

Why is the ocean so important to the people of the Pacific Islands? The ocean is a big part of everyday life. It is, in many ways, part of their home. It provides a source of food and a way to get around.

The Bounty of the Ocean

How did the Pacific Islanders find food in the ocean? Islanders fished with nets, baskets, and hooks. Sometimes they fished from shore, and sometimes they fished from boats. Some Samoan fishhooks were made from snail shells. Fish were and are a very important source of food for Pacific Islanders.

Canoes

The first Pacific explorers traveled on boats. They sailed thousands of miles on canoes. There are no canoes from that time left in the world. But new canoes exist that are similar. And we can make some guesses about what the early canoes were like. The most important boat for long trips was the **double-hulled canoe**. This canoe was built to make many long voyages.

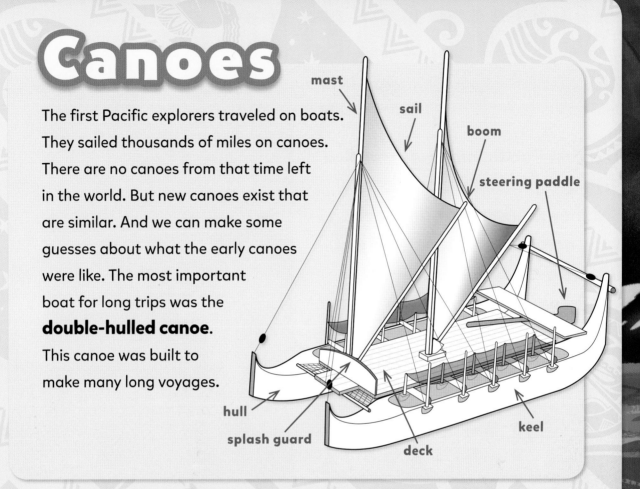

mast

sail

boom

steering paddle

hull

splash guard

deck

keel

The Great Connector

The Pacific Islands are spread out across the ocean. They are far from one another, and even farther from other parts of the world. It's easy to think that the ocean keeps the islands isolated. But that's not how the people of the Pacific Islands think. They see the ocean as the great connector. It connects the islands to one another. It connects the islands to the world.

WAYFINDING

The first Pacific Islanders traveled very far on their canoes. But how did they **navigate**, or find their way, across open ocean? Or from island to island? They practiced wayfinding!

Navigating Without Instruments

Early Pacific Islanders didn't have most of the tools that we have today to find our way. They didn't have compasses. They didn't have sextants, which are special instruments to measure distance. The earliest explorers didn't even have maps! So how did they do it? In Micronesia early explorers trained using a stick chart. The stick chart mapped where islands and currents were. Wayfinders used their eyes and ears and studied the ocean for years. They remembered what they learned and passed their knowledge on, often through song.

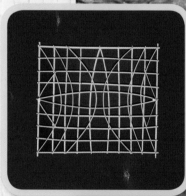

Currents, Waves, and Colors

Island voyagers used the ocean itself to find their way. They learned to recognize the changing ocean currents. They studied the speed and size of ocean waves. They even looked at the changing color of the ocean!

Red-billed tropic bird

Ocean Animals

The early voyagers watched traveling animals. They learned the flight paths of local birds. When the birds flew overhead, this gave them information. They watched for sea turtles and the direction they were traveling. They noticed how fast they were swimming. All of these were important clues to the wayfinders.

Green sea turtle

USING THE SKY TO GET AROUND

The first Pacific explorers didn't just look down at the ocean when they were wayfinding. They also looked up at the sky!

The Day Sky

Early Pacific Islanders realized that clouds move toward land in a special V shape. They also noticed that clouds changed color when they were over land. Clouds were brighter over a white sand beach. Clouds were darker over a forest or a black sand beach. Early wayfinders also used the sun to find their way. They knew that the sun rises in the east and sets in the west. That helped them know where they were going.

The Night Sky

Early voyagers didn't navigate only during the day. They also used the stars at night to find their way. Wayfinders watched the positions of the stars move in the sky. As stars rose and fell in the sky, wayfinders could tell which direction they were heading.

Watching the Wind

wind flag

Wayfinders paid close attention to the wind. Some of them made wind flags and tied them to their canoes. The flags, made of feather and bark, would point in the direction the wind was blowing.

Memory and Observation

Wayfinders had amazing memories. They had to memorize stars, wind patterns, wave shapes, ocean colors, currents, and more. Not only that—they had to pay attention all the time. They had to notice every change in the wind, the sky, and the ocean.

EARLY PACIFIC ISLANDERS AND EXPLORATION

We've learned that people didn't always live on the Pacific Islands. They traveled there! That's a long trip across the ocean. Let's learn more about these adventurous explorers.

Where Did They Come From?

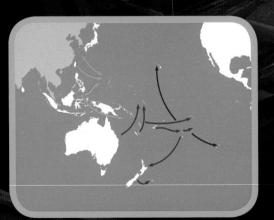

We have no remaining records written by the first Pacific Islanders. What we know comes from stories like Gramma Tala's. We've also learned from petroglyphs and songs. We can't be sure about the details of the first explorers. We think that many thousands of years ago, they sailed from Southeast Asia. They settled in New Guinea. Much later, they sailed east to the other Pacific Islands.

The Journey

The journey east would have taken months. The wayfinders brought plants and animals with them. They brought whatever they needed to start a new life. They did not know what they would find.

A Long Pause

After thousands of years of exploration, early islanders took a long break from exploring. Just how long this break lasted is not known for sure. Some historians think it may have lasted as long as one thousand years. Why did early islanders stop sailing east? We don't know! We also don't know why they started again about two thousand years ago.

MAUI STORIES

Gramma Tala knows a lot of stories about the demigod Maui. Different islands have different stories about him.

Tongan Maui

The Tongans say that Maui carries the weight of the earth on his shoulders. When Maui sleeps and nods his head, it causes earthquakes!

Māori Māui

The **indigenous**, or native, people of New Zealand are called the **Māori**. The Māori tell stories about Māui too. They say he had a magic fishhook. He used this fishhook to pull the island of New Zealand up from the sea. The Māori give thanks to Māui for giving them their home.

Hawai'ian Maui

In Hawai'i, there are many legends about Maui. One says he caught the sun with a rope. He made it slow down so that the days would be longer. Another says he lifted up the sky with his arms! A third says that he discovered the secret of fire. He gave it to people so they could cook and stay warm.

MORE TALES FROM THE ISLANDS

Maui isn't the only god in the Pacific! There are many stories about other gods that are important to the people of the Pacific Islands, their cultures, and their stories.

Ocean Gods

In Hawai'i, people worshipped many gods. They called them **akua**. Maui is just one akua of many. There is also **Kanaloa**, god of the ocean. There is **Kāne**, god of creation, sunlight, and freshwater. There is **Lono**, god of farming and rain. Each akua is in charge of a different part of life.

Rangi and Papa

In New Zealand, the Māori told stories about the beginning of the world. In their stories, the world began with **Rangi** and **Papa**. Rangi is the father of the world. He is the sky. Papa is the mother of the world. She is the earth. In the beginning, Rangi and Papa held each other tight, and everything was dark.

Tāne

Rangi and Papa had many sons. One of them was **Tāne**. Tāne is the god of forests and birds. One day Tāne pushed his parents apart. Rangi stays in the sky. Papa stays on the earth. This is how life began. When Rangi misses Papa, he cries. His tears are the rain.

ISLAND CHALLENGES

The Pacific Islands are full of plants, animals, and people. They are also full of stories. Pacific Islanders have lived in their homes for thousands of years. At times, though, they face challenges.

Living in Harmony

Each of the Pacific Islands is like a small world. All the plants, animals, and people have to live together. This is called an **ecosystem**. It takes a special balance for everyone to be happy. People cut down trees to make *fale*. Animals eat plants. People feed the animals. It is important to think about all the living things in your small world.

Water

The Pacific Islands are surrounded by water. But you can't drink the ocean. People need clean freshwater to drink. Some islands don't have very much freshwater. Plants and animals need water too. Water is a precious resource.

Keeping the Ocean Stories Alive

Gramma Tala learned the stories she tells from her parents and her grandparents. She passes them on to Moana. Moana will one day pass them on to the next generation. These stories are an important part of what makes the Pacific Islands special. By telling stories to one another, we keep the stories alive!

GOODBYE FOR NOW!

We've learned so much about the Pacific Islands Moana and her friends call home. We've learned about wayfinding and how important the currents, wind, sun, stars, and ocean animals were to early navigators. We've learned that Pacific Islanders have deep musical cultures filled with drums, song, dances, and ceremonies. And we've learned that the ocean is the great connector that bridges the islands to one another and to the world.

As they say in Samoa, Tahiti, and Fiji: *Tōfā! Nana! Moce!* In other words:

Goodbye! Come visit soon!

GLOSSARY

akua: Hawai'ian gods

Aotearoa: a country in Polynesia, also called New Zealand

canoe: a seaworthy vessel built by Pacific Islanders for traveling on the ocean

chief: a person elected to lead a family or village

climate: the usual weather in a place

coconut palm: a kind of palm tree that produces coconuts

conch shell: the shell of an ocean animal that can be used as a musical instrument

double-hulled canoe: a canoe made up of two canoes tied together

Easter Island: an island in eastern Polynesia originally called Rapa Nui

ecosystem: all the living things in a place

fale: a traditional house in Tonga or Samoa

fauna: all the animals in a place

fern: a plant with big leaves and no flowers

Fiji: a country of mixed Melanesian and Polynesian cultures. Originally called Viti, Fiji is made up of 330 islands.

flora: all the plants in a place

grassland: land covered in grasses and not trees

Ha'amonga 'a Maui: a monument in Tonga

Hawai'i: a group of islands in Polynesia; also a state of the United States

headdress: a ceremonial covering worn on the head

indigenous: originally living in a place

Kanaloa: Hawai'ian god of the ocean

Kāne: Hawai'ian god of freshwater and sunlight

lali: a long drum from Fiji

Lono: Hawai'ian god of farming and rain

malae: a village square in Samoa

mangrove: a tree that grows next to salt water

Māori: the indigenous people of New Zealand

Marquesas Islands: a group of islands in French Polynesia

Marshall Islands: a group of more than one thousand islands about halfway between Hawai'i and Australia

Melanesia: a group of western Pacific Islands that includes Fiji, Papua New Guinea, and the Solomon Islands

Micronesia: a group of northwestern Pacific Islands that includes Kiribati and the Marshall Islands

moai: one of more than nine hundred statues with large heads spread all over Rapa Nui

native: originally from a place

navigate: to find one's way from one place to another

New Zealand: a country in Polynesia originally called Aotearoa

non-native: brought to a place from somewhere else

nose flute: a musical instrument played with the nose

Oceania: another name for the Pacific Islands

oral history: stories that are passed from generation to generation by word of mouth

Pacific Islands: the countries of the Pacific Ocean

Pacific Ocean: the largest ocean in the world

pahu: a Polynesian drum made from sharkskin and the trunk of a coconut tree

panpipes: a musical instrument made of different-length tubes that are blown across

Papa: Māori goddess of the earth and mother of the world

Papua New Guinea: a country in Melanesia

petroglyph: a rock drawing

Polynesia: a group of Pacific Islands that includes Hawai'i, New Zealand, and Samoa

rain forest: a forest where it rains a lot

Rangi: Māori god of the sky and father of the world

Rapa Nui: an island in eastern Polynesia, also called Easter Island

rattles: a musical instrument that makes a rattling sound

Samoa: a group of islands in south central Polynesia

seabird: a bird that feeds in the ocean

Tahiti: the largest and most populated island in French Polynesia

Tāne: Māori god of forests and birds; son of Rangi and Papa

tapa: a cloth made from wild hibiscus bark

tattoo: a permanent marking or drawing on the skin made by tapping tools that apply ink

Tonga: a Polynesian country made up of 171 islands

tuiga: a ceremonial Samoan headdress

wayfinding: the technique developed by early Pacific Islanders to travel across the ocean

INDEX

PHOTO CREDITS

All photos are listed by page number from top to bottom.